Penguin Modern Poets
VOLUME 2

Carol Ann Duffy was born in Glasgow in 1955, grew up in Stafford-shire and attended university in Liverpool before moving to London, where she now works as a freelance writer. She has published four collections of poems and has received many awards. In 1984 she won an Eric Gregory Award and has been recipient of a Scottish Arts Council Book Award for her collections *Standing Female Nude* and *The Other Country*. Carol Ann Duffy was awarded a Somerset Maugham Award in 1988 for her collection *Selling Manhattan*, the Dylan Thomas Award in 1989 and a Cholmondeley Award in 1992. Her most recent collection of poems, *Mean Time*, which also received a Scottish Arts Council Book Award, won the 1993 Whitbread Award for poetry and the Forward Prize.

Vicki Feaver was born in Nottingham in 1943. She initially studied music but later took a First in English at University College London. She now leads an MA in Creative Writing at the Chichester Institute. Her own publications include two volumes of poetry, *Close Relatives* and *The Handless Maiden*. In 1993 she was awarded a Hawthornden Fellowship and a Forward Prize for her poem 'Judith'.

Eavan Boland was born in Dublin in 1944 and was educated in London and New York. She graduated from Trinity College in Dublin, where she taught briefly. She has published seven volumes of poetry, including *The Journey* (1987), *Outside History* (1990) and *In a Time of Violence* (1994), all of them being Poetry Book Society Choices. She has been a writer-in-residence at Trinity College and University College Dublin and at the National Maternity Hospital. She lives in Dublin with her husband and two daughters. Her collection of poetry, *In a Time of Violence*, received the Literature award of the Ireland-American Foundation, a Lannan Award for Poetry and was shortlisted for the T. S. Eliot Poetry Prize.

Penguin Modern Poets

VOLUME 2

CAROL ANN DUFFY

VICKI FEAVER

EAVAN BOLAND

PENGUIN BOOKS

Published by the Penguin Group
Penguin Books Ltd, 27 Wrights Lane, London w8 5tz, England
Penguin Books USA Inc., 375 Hudson Street, New York, New York 10014, USA
Penguin Books Australia Ltd, Ringwood, Victoria, Australia
Penguin Books Canada Ltd, 10 Alcorn Avenue, Toronto, Ontario, Canada m4v 3b2
Penguin Books (NZ) Ltd, 182–190 Wairau Road, Auckland 10, New Zealand

Penguin Books Ltd, Registered Offices: Harmondsworth, Middlesex, England

10 9 8 7 6 5

This selection first published 1995

Filmset by Datix International Limited, Bungay, Suffolk
Printed in England by Clays Ltd, St Ives plc
Set in 10.5/14pt Monophoto Garamond

Contents

Carol Ann Duffy

Head of English

Today we have a poet in the class.
A real live poet with a published book.
Notice the inkstained fingers girls. Perhaps
we're going to witness verse hot from the press.
Who knows. Please show your appreciation
by clapping. Not too loud. Now

sit up straight and listen. Remember
the lesson on assonance, for not all poems,
sadly, rhyme these days. Still. Never mind.
Whispering's, as always, out of bounds –
but do feel free to raise some questions.
After all, we're paying forty pounds.

Those of you with English Second Language
see me after break. We're fortunate
to have this person in our midst.
Season of mists and so on and so forth.
I've written quite a bit of poetry myself,
am doing Kipling with the Lower Fourth.

Right. That's enough from me. On with the Muse.
Open a window at the back. We don't
want winds of change about the place.
Take notes, but don't write reams. Just an essay
on the poet's themes. Fine. Off we go.
Convince us that there's something we don't know.

Well. Really. Run along now girls. I'm sure
that gave an insight to an outside view.
Applause will do. Thank you
very much for coming here today. Lunch
in the hall? Do hang about. Unfortunately
I have to dash. Tracey will show you out.

In Mrs Tilscher's Class

You could travel up the Blue Nile
with your finger, tracing the route
while Mrs Tilscher chanted the scenery.
Tana. Ethiopia. Khartoum. Aswân.
That for an hour, then a skittle of milk
and the chalky Pyramids rubbed into dust.
A window opened with a long pole.
The laugh of a bell swung by a running child.

This was better than home. Enthralling books.
The classroom glowed like a sweetshop.
Sugar paper. Coloured shapes. Brady and Hindley
faded, like the faint, uneasy smudge of a mistake.
Mrs Tilscher loved you. Some mornings, you found
she'd left a good gold star by your name.
The scent of a pencil slowly, carefully, shaved.
A xylophone's nonsense heard from another form.

Over the Easter term, the inky tadpoles changed
from commas into exclamation marks. Three frogs
hopped in the playground, freed by a dunce,
followed by a line of kids, jumping and croaking
away from the lunch queue. A rough boy
told you how you were born. You kicked him, but stared
at your parents, appalled, when you got back home.

That feverish July, the air tasted of electricity.
A tangible alarm made you always untidy, hot,
fractious under the heavy, sexy sky. You asked her
how you were born and Mrs Tilscher smiled,
then turned away. Reports were handed out.
You ran through the gates, impatient to be grown,
as the sky split open into a thunderstorm.

The Good Teachers

You run round the back to be in it again.
No bigger than your thumbs, those virtuous women
size you up from the front row. Soon now,
Miss Ross will take you for double History.
You breathe on the glass, making a ghost of her, say
South Sea Bubble Defenestration of Prague.

You love Miss Pirie. So much, you are top
of her class. So much, you need two of you
to stare out from the year, serious, passionate.
The River's Tale by Rudyard Kipling by heart.
Her kind intelligent green eye. Her cruel blue one.
You are making a poem up for her in your head.

But not Miss Sheridan. Comment vous appelez.
But not Miss Appleby. Equal to the square
of the other two sides. Never Miss Webb.
Dar es Salaam. Kilimanjaro. Look. The good teachers
swish down the corridor in long, brown skirts,
snobbish and proud and clean and qualified.

And they've got your number. You roll the waistband
of your skirt over and over, all leg, all
dumb insolence, smoke-rings. You won't pass.
You could do better. But there's the wall you climb
into dancing, lovebites, marriage, the Cheltenham
and Gloucester, today. The day you'll be sorry one day.

The Virgin Punishing the Infant

After the painting by Max Ernst

He spoke early. Not the *goo goo goo* of infancy,
but *I am God*. Joseph kept away, carving himself
a silent Pinocchio out in the workshed. He said
he was a simple man and hadn't dreamed of this.

She grew anxious in that second year, would stare
at stars saying *Gabriel? Gabriel?* Your guess.
The village gossiped in the sun. The child was solitary,
his wide and solemn eyes could fill your head.

After he walked, our normal children crawled. Our wives
were first resentful, then superior. Mary's child
would bring her sorrow . . . better far to have a son
who gurgled nonsense at your breast. *Googoo. Googoo.*

But I am God. We heard him through the window,
heard the smacks which made us peep. What we saw
was commonplace enough. But afterwards, we wondered
why the infant did not cry. And why the Mother did.

Litany

The soundtrack then was a litany – *candlewick*
bedspread three piece suite display cabinet –
and stiff-haired wives balanced their red smiles,
passing the catalogue. *Pyrex*. A tiny ladder
ran up Mrs Barr's American Tan leg, sly
like a rumour. Language embarrassed them.

The terrible marriages crackled, cellophane
round polyester shirts, and then The Lounge
would seem to bristle with eyes, hard
as the bright stones in engagement rings,
and sharp hands poised over biscuits as a word
was spelled out. An embarrassing word, broken

to bits, which tensed the air like an accident.
This was the code I learnt at my mother's knee,
    pretending
to read, where no one had cancer, or sex, or debts,
and certainly not leukaemia, which no one could spell.
The year a mass grave of wasps bobbed in a jam-jar;
a butterfly stammered itself in my curious hands.

A boy in the playground, I said, *told me*
to fuck off; and a thrilled, malicious pause
salted my tongue like an imminent storm. Then
uproar. *I'm sorry, Mrs Barr, Mrs Hunt, Mrs Emery,*
sorry, Mrs Raine. Yes, I can summon their names.
My mother's mute shame. The taste of soap.

Stafford Afternoons

Only there, the afternoons could suddenly pause
and when I looked up from lacing my shoe
a long road held no one, the gardens were empty,
an ice-cream van chimed and dwindled away.

On the motorway bridge, I waved at windscreens,
oddly hurt by the blurred waves back, the speed.
So I let a horse in the noisy field sponge at my palm
and invented, in colour, a vivid lie for us both.

In a cul-de-sac, a strange boy threw a stone.
I crawled through a hedge into long grass
at the edge of a small wood, lonely and thrilled.
The green silence gulped once and swallowed me whole.

I knew it was dangerous. The way the trees
drew sly faces from light and shade, the wood
let out its sticky breath on the back of my neck,
and flowering nettles gathered spit in their throats.

Too late. *Touch*, said the long-haired man
who stood, legs apart, by a silver birch
with a living, purple root in his hand. The sight
made sound rush back; birds, a distant lawnmower,

his hoarse, frightful endearments as I backed away
then ran all the way home; into a game
where children scattered and shrieked
and time fell from the sky like a red ball.

When the sky showed both a sun and a moon
I went off with the twins. *Come home with us,*
they'd said to me, alone in the street
with my skipping rope, bells in the handles.

One twin skipped ahead, chiming and tinkling,
the other walked beside me, too close, close enough
for her sugary breath to tickle my cheek. The gardens
lengthened and deepened. They led me away;

smiling at the same time, making me
eat pink words on identical lovehearts. *Hi Chum.*
There was something odd that drew the eye
to their socks. Only their ribbons differed.

In here. When we got to their house
I was scared. Their four eager narrow eyes. Then
both of them swore, pulling me, as I sobbed, to
their wooden blue gate, its small white 2.

When I slipped, the gravel bit at my knees,
peppery. *There's two of us.* And when I ran
they chased me, yanking me back by the hair;
and what they did to me then they did to me twice.

The Cliché Kid

I need help, Doc, and bad; I can't forget
the rustle of my father's ballgown as he bent
to say goodnight to me, his kiss, his French scent . . .

Give me a shot of something. Or the sound of Ma
and her pals up late, boozing, dealing the cards.
Big Bertha pissing out from the porch under the stars . . .

It gets worse. Chalkdust. The old schoolroom empty.
This kid so unpopular even my imaginary friend left me
for another child. I'm screwed up, Doc, jumpy . . .

Distraught in autumn, kneeling under the chestnut trees,
seeing childhood in the conkers through my tears.
Bonkers. And me so butch in my boots down the macho
        bars . . .

Give me a break. Don't let me pine for that first love,
that faint down on the cheeks, that easy laugh
in my ears, in my lonesome heart, the day that I had to
        leave . . .

Sweet Jesus, Doc, I worry I'll miss when a long time dead
the smell the smell the smell of the baby's head,
the fresh-baked grass, dammit, the new-mown bread . . .

The Captain of the 1964 *Top of the Form* Team

Do Wah Diddy Diddy, Baby Love, Oh Pretty Woman
were in the Top Ten that month, October, and the Beatles
were everywhere else. I can give you the B-side
of the Supremes one. Hang on. *Come See About Me?*
I lived in a kind of fizzing hope. Gargling
with Vimto. The clever smell of my satchel. Convent girls.
I pulled my hair forward with a steel comb that I blew
like Mick, my lips numb as a two-hour snog.

No snags. The Nile rises in April. Blue and White.
The humming-bird's song is made by its wings, which
    beat
so fast that they blur in flight. I knew the capitals,
the Kings and Queens, the dates. In class, the white sleeve
of my shirt saluted again and again. *Sir! . . . Correct.*
Later, I whooped at the side of my bike, a cowboy,
mounted it running in one jump. I sped down Dyke Hill,
no hands, famous, learning, *dominus domine dominum.*

Dave Dee Dozy . . . Try me. Come on. My mother kept my
    mascot Gonk
on the TV set for a year. And the photograph. I look
so brainy you'd think I'd just had a bath. The blazer.
The badge. The tie. The first chord of *A Hard Day's Night*
loud in my head. I ran to the Spinney in my prize shoes,
up Churchill Way, up Nelson Drive, over pink pavements
that girls chalked on, in a blue evening; and I stamped
the paw prints of badgers and skunks in the mud. My
    country.

I want it back. The Captain. The one with all the answers.
  Bzz.
My name was in red on Lucille Green's jotter. I smiled
as wide as a child who went missing on the way home
from school. The keeny. I say to my stale wife
Six hits by Dusty Springfield. I say to my boss *A pint!*
How can we know the dancer from the dance? Nobody.
My thick kids wince. *Name the Prime Minister of Rhodesia.*
My country. *How many florins in a pound?*

Translating the English, 1989

'. . . and much of the poetry, alas, is lost in translation . . .'

Welcome to my country! We have here Edwina Currie
and The Sun newspaper. Much excitement.
Also the weather has been most improving
even in February. Daffodils. (Wordsworth. Up North.) If you like
Shakespeare or even Opera we have too the Black Market.
For two hundred quids we are talking Les Miserables,
nods being as good as winks. Don't eat the eggs.
Wheel-clamp. Dogs. Vagrants. A tour of our wonderful
capital city is not to be missed. The Fergie,
The Princess Di and the football hooligan, truly you will
like it here, Squire. Also we can be talking crack, smack
and Carling Black Label if we are so inclined. Don't
drink the H_2O. All very proud we now have
a green Prime Minister. What colour yours? Binbags.
You will be knowing of Charles Dickens and Terry Wogan
and Scotland. All this can be arranged for cash no questions.
Ireland not on. Fish and chips and the Official Secrets Act
second to none. Here we go. We are liking
a smashing good time like estate agents and Neighbours,
also Brookside for we are allowed four Channels.
How many you have? Last night of Proms. Andrew
Lloyd-Webber. Jeffrey Archer. Plenty culture you will be agreeing.
Also history and buildings. The Houses of Lords. Docklands.
Many thrills and high interest rates for own good. Muggers.
Much lead in petrol. Filth. Rule Britannia and child abuse.
Electronic tagging, Boss, ten pints and plenty rape. Queen Mum.
Channel Tunnel. You get here fast no problem to my country
my country my country welcome welcome welcome.

Like Earning a Living

What's an elephant like? I say
to the slack-mouthed girl
who answers back, a trainee ventriloquist,
then smirks at Donna. She dunno.
Nor does the youth with the face.
And what would that say, fingered?
I know. Video. Big Mac. Lager. Lager.
What like's a wart-hog? Come on.

Ambition. Rage. Boredom. Spite. How
do they taste, smell, sound?
Nobody cares. Jason doesn't. Nor does his dad.
He met a poet. Didn't know it. Uungh.
What would that aftershave say
if it could think? What colour's the future?

Somewhere in England, Major-Balls,
the long afternoon empties of air, meaning, energy, point.
Kin-L. There just aren't the words for it.
Darren. Paul. Kelly. Marie. What's it like? Mike?

Like earning a living.
Earning a living like.

Phone-In

Call her about my age. Single. She doesn't like
the crimes that go on in Great Britain under cover
of night, in broad daylight even. She telephones
the radio and talks to dark cars on the ringroad,
conversion flats, an all-night café amber in the rain;
her voice surprising itself with oddness, risk,
into an accent half an inch from her own.

She can't express it, of course, there isn't the time,
and, anyway, she was better at Maths. ✓.
But if she thinks of her journey from home to work
to home, she sees it in words written out
in violent paint on walls, buildings, tube-trains,
loathes it. Don't Pay. Not Guilty. Pigs. Worse.
Words on the litter she scuffs on the way to the bank,

one piece the front page of a tabloid
demanding the rope for a bastard who killed a kid.
It is one a.m. She is calling from Tufnell Park
where she has a life that a careful listener can
almost hear. She sits in her yellow kitchen
trying to explain to the darkness outside
that the country has changed. Faintly, she tastes
the past on her tongue like the end of a mint,

where it was *decent*, showed *respect* and *care*;
she sounds like she looks as though *better* wouldn't melt
in her mouth. The D J hears what she's saying.
Later, the News. Then, an exclusive interview
in which Baroness Thatcher shows where she feels we all
went wrong. Before all that, to cheer up Carol in N19,
and it does, a golden oldie from Don McLean.

Fraud

Firstly, I changed my name
to that of a youth I knew for sure had bought it in 1940,
   Rotterdam.
Private M.
I was my own poem,
pseudonym,
rule of thumb.
What was my aim?
To change from a bum
to a billionaire. I spoke the English. Mine was a scam
involving pensions, papers, politicians in-and-out of their
   pram.
And I was to blame.

For what? There's a gnome
in Zurich knows more than people assume.
There's a military man, Jerusalem
way, keeping schtum.
Then there's Him –
for whom
I paid for a butch and femme
to make him come.
And all of the crème
de la crème
considered me scum.

Poverty's dumb.
Take it from me, Sonny Jim,
learn to lie in the mother-tongue of the motherfucker you
   want to charm.

They're all the same,
turning their wide blind eyes to crime.
And who gives a damn
when the keys to a second home
are pressed in his palm,
or Polaroids of a Night of Shame
with a Boy on the Game
are passed his way at the A.G.M.?

So read my lips. Mo-ney. Pow-er. Fame.
And had I been asked, in my time,
in my puce and prosperous prime,
if I recalled the crumbling slum
of my Daddy's home,
if I was a shit, a sham,
if I'd done immeasurable harm,
I could have replied with a dream:
the water that night was calm
and with my enormous mouth, in bubbles and blood and
    phlegm,
I gargled my name.

The Biographer

Because you are dead,
I stand at your desk,
my fingers caressing the grooves in the wood
your initials made;
and I manage a quote,
echo one of your lines in the small, blue room
where an early daguerreotype shows you
excitedly staring out
from behind your face,
the thing that made you yourself
still visibly there,
like a hood and a cloak of light.
The first four words that I write are your name.

I'm a passionate man
with a big advance
who's loved your work since he was a boy;
but the night
I slept alone in your bed,
the end of a fire going out in the grate,
I came awake –
certain, had we ever met,
you wouldn't have wanted me,
or needed me,
would barely have noticed me at all.
Guilt and rage
hardened me then,

and later I felt your dislike
chilling the air
as I drifted away.
Your wallpaper green and crimson and gold.

How close can I get
to the sound of your voice
which Emma Elizabeth Hibbert described –
lively, eager and lightly-pitched,
with none of the later, bitter edge.
Cockney, a little.
In London Town,
the faces you wrote
leer and gape and plead at my feet.
Once, high on Hungerford Bridge,
a stew and tangle of rags, sniffed by a dog, stood, spoke,
spat at the shadow I cast,
at the meagre shadow I cast in my time.
I heard the faraway bells of St Paul's as I ran.

Maestro. Monster. Mummy's Boy.
My Main Man.
I write you and write you for five hard years.
I have an affair with a thespian girl –
you would have approved –
then I snivel home to my wife.
Her poems and jam.
Her forgiveness.
Her violent love.
And this is a life.
I print it out.
I print it out.
In all of your mirrors, my face;
with its smallish, its quizzical eyes,
its cheekbones, its sexy jaw,
its talentless, dustjacket smile.

The Legend

Some say it was seven tons of meat in a thick black hide
you could build a boat from, stayed close to the river
on the flipside of the sun where the giant forests were.

Had shy, old eyes. You'd need both those hands for *one*.
Maybe. Walked in placid herds under a jungly, sweating
     roof
just breathing; a dry electric wind you could hear a mile
     off.

Huge feet. Some say if it rained you could fish in a
     footprint,
fruit fell when it passed. It moved, food happened, simple.
You think of a warm, inky cave and you got its mouth all
     right.

You dream up a yard of sandpaper, damp, you're talking
     tongue.
Eat? Its own weight in a week. And water. Some say
the sweat steamed from its back in small grey clouds.

But *big*. Enormous. Spine like the mast on a galleon.
Ears like sails gasping for a wind. You picture
a rope you could hang a man from, you're seeing its tail.

Tusks like bannisters. I almost believe myself. Can you
drum up a roar as wide as a continent, a deep hot note
that bellowed out and belonged to the melting air? You
     got it.

But people have always lied! You know some say it had a
   trunk
like a soft telescope, that it looked up along it at the sky
and balanced a bright, gone star on the end, and it died.

A Healthy Meal

The gourmet tastes the secret dreams of cows
tossed lightly in garlic. Behind the green door, swish
of oxtails languish on an earthen dish. Here are
wishbones and pinkies; fingerbowls will absolve guilt.

Capped teeth chatter to a kidney or at the breast
of something which once flew. These hearts knew
no love and on their beds of saffron rice they lie
beyond reproach. What is the claret like? Blood.

On table six, the language of tongues is braised
in armagnac. The woman chewing suckling pig
must sleep with her husband later. Leg,
saddle and breast bleat against pure white cloth.

Alter *calf* to *veal* in four attempts. This is
the power of words; knife, tripe, lights, charcuterie.
A fat man orders his *rare* and a fine sweat
bastes his face. There are napkins to wipe the evidence

and sauces to gag the groans of abattoirs. The menu
lists the recent dead in French, from which they order
offal, poultry, fish. Meat flops in the jowls. Belch.
Death moves in the bowels. You are what you eat.

Foreign

Imagine living in a strange, dark city for twenty years.
There are some dismal dwellings on the east side
and one of them is yours. On the landing, you hear
your foreign accent echo down the stairs. You think
in a language of your own and talk in theirs.

Then you are writing home. The voice in your head
recites the letter in a local dialect; behind that
is the sound of your mother singing to you,
all that time ago, and now you do not know
why your eyes are watering and what's the word for this.

You use the public transport. Work. Sleep. Imagine one
     night
you saw a name for yourself sprayed in red
against a brick wall. A hate name. Red like blood.
It is snowing on the streets, under the neon lights,
as if this place were coming to bits before your eyes.

And in the delicatessen, from time to time, the coins
in your palm will not translate. Inarticulate,
because this is not home, you point at fruit. Imagine
that one of you says *Me not know what these people mean.*
It like they only go to bed and dream. Imagine that.

Plainsong

Stop. Along this path, in phrases of light,
trees sing their leaves. No Midas touch
has turned the wood to gold, late in the year
when you pass by, suddenly sad, straining
to remember something you're sure you knew.

Listening. The words you have for things die
in your heart, but grasses are plainsong,
patiently chanting the circles you cannot repeat
or understand. This is your homeland,
Lost One, Stranger who speaks with tears.

It is almost impossible to be here and yet
you kneel, no one's child, absolved by late sun
through the branches of a wood, distantly
the evening bell reminding you, *Home, Home,
Home*, and the stone in your palm telling the time.

Standing Female Nude

Six hours like this for a few francs.
Belly nipple arse in the window light,
he drains the colour from me. Further to the right,
Madame. And do try to be still.
I shall be represented analytically and hung
in great museums. The bourgeoisie will coo
at such an image of a river-whore. They call it Art.

Maybe. He is concerned with volume, space.
I with the next meal. You're getting thin,
Madame, this is not good. My breasts hang
slightly low, the studio is cold. In the tea-leaves
I can see the Queen of England gazing
on my shape. Magnificent, she murmurs,
moving on. It makes me laugh. His name

is Georges. They tell me he's a genius.
There are times he does not concentrate
and stiffens for my warmth.
He possesses me on canvas as he dips the brush
repeatedly into the paint. Little man,
you've not the money for the arts I sell.
Both poor, we make our living how we can.

I ask him Why do you do this? Because
I have to. There's no choice. Don't talk.
My smile confuses him. These artists
take themselves too seriously. At night I fill myself
with wine and dance around the bars. When it's finished
he shows me proudly, lights a cigarette. I say
Twelve francs and get my shawl. It does not look like me.

Warming Her Pearls

For Judith Radstone

Next to my own skin, her pearls. My mistress
bids me wear them, warm them, until evening
when I'll brush her hair. At six, I place them
round her cool, white throat. All day I think of her,

resting in the Yellow Room, contemplating silk
or taffeta, which gown tonight? She fans herself
whilst I work willingly, my slow heat entering
each pearl. Slack on my neck, her rope.

She's beautiful. I dream about her
in my attic bed; picture her dancing
with tall men, puzzled by my faint, persistent scent
beneath her French perfume, her milky stones.

I dust her shoulders with a rabbit's foot,
watch the soft blush seep through her skin
like an indolent sigh. In her looking-glass
my red lips part as though I want to speak.

Full moon. Her carriage brings her home. I see
her every movement in my head . . . Undressing,
taking off her jewels, her slim hand reaching
for the case, slipping naked into bed, the way

she always does . . . And I lie here awake,
knowing the pearls are cooling even now
in the room where my mistress sleeps. All night
I feel their absence and I burn.

Who Loves You

I worry about you travelling in those mystical machines.
Every day people fall from the clouds, dead.
Breathe in and out and in and out easy.
Safety, safely, safe home.

Your photograph is in the fridge, smiles when the light
   comes on.
All the time people are burnt in the public places.
Rest where the cool trees drop to a gentle shade.
Safety, safely, safe home.

Don't lie down on the sands where the hole in the sky is.
Too many people being gnawed to shreds.
Send me your voice however it comes across oceans.
Safety, safely, safe home.

The loveless men and homeless boys are out there and
   angry.
Nightly people end their lives in the shortcut.
Walk in the light, steadily hurry towards me.
Safety, safely, safe home. (Who loves you?)
Safety, safely, safe home.

The Windows

How do you earn a life going on
behind yellow windows, writing at night
the Latin names of plants for a garden,
opening the front door to a wet dog?

Those you love forgive you, clearly,
with steaming casseroles and red wine.
It's the same film down all the suburban streets,
It's A Wonderful Life. How do you learn it?

What you hear – the doorbell's familiar chime.
What you touch – the clean, warm towels.
What you see what you smell what you taste
all tangible to the stranger passing your gate.

There you are again, in a room where those early hyacinths
surely sweeten the air, and the right words wait
in the dictionaries, on the tip of the tongue you touch
in a kiss, drawing your crimson curtains now

against dark hours. And again, in a kitchen,
the window ajar, sometimes the sound of your radio
or the scent of your food, and a cat in your arms,
a child in your arms, a lover. Such vivid flowers.

Twinned

I have been wined and dined
in the town with which this one is twinned.
The people were kind, I found.

I have walked hand-in-hand,
scraped two names and a heart with a stick on the sand
in the town with which this one is twinned,
become over-soon over-fond.

And stayed in my room when it rained,
hearing the wind,
with love love love on my mind,
in the town with which this one is twinned,
and pined.

So one day I left it behind –
what little I owned,
whatever I'd gained;
composed a letter to send,
in the town with which this one is twinned,
to a practical friend.

Then went to see what I'd find
in a different land
where the life, so they said, was grand;
for I had nothing particular planned,
had only the future once read from the palm of my hand
in the town with which this one is twinned,
and a broken heart for somebody somewhere to mend.

The Way My Mother Speaks

I say her phrases to myself
in my head
or under the shallows of my breath,
restful shapes moving.
The day and ever. The day and ever.

The train this slow evening
goes down England
browsing for the right sky,
too blue swapped for a cool grey.
For miles I have been saying
What like is it
the way I say things when I think.
Nothing is silent. Nothing is not silent.
What like is it.

Only tonight
I am happy and sad
like a child
who stood at the end of summer
and dipped a net
in a green, erotic pond. *The day
and ever. The day and ever.*
I am homesick, free, in love
with the way my mother speaks.

Mrs Midas

It was late September. I'd just poured a glass of wine, begun
to unwind, while the vegetables cooked. The kitchen
filled with the smell of itself, relaxed, its steamy breath
gently blanching the windows. So I opened one,
then with my fingers wiped the other's glass like a brow.
He was standing under the pear-tree snapping a twig.

Now the garden was long and the visibility poor, the way
the dark of the ground seems to drink the light of the sky,
but that twig in his hand was gold. And then he plucked
a pear from a branch, we grew Fondante d'Automne,
and it sat in his palm like a light-bulb. On.
I thought to myself, Is he putting fairy lights in the tree?

He came into the house. The doorknobs gleamed.
He drew the blinds. You know the mind; I thought of
the Field of the Cloth of Gold and of Miss Macready.
He sat in that chair like a king on a burnished throne.
The look on his face was strange, wild, vain; I said,
What in the name of God is going on? He started to laugh.

I served up the meal. For starters, corn on the cob.
Within seconds he was spitting out the teeth of the rich.
He toyed with his spoon, then mine, then with the knives,
     the forks.
He asked where was the wine. I poured with a shaking hand,
a fragrant, bone-dry white from Italy, then watched
as he picked up the glass, goblet, golden chalice, drank.

It was then that I started to scream. He sank to his knees.
After we'd both calmed down, I finished the wine
on my own, hearing him out. I made him sit
on the other side of the room and keep his hands to
    himself.
I locked the cat in the cellar. I moved the phone.
The toilet I didn't mind. I couldn't believe my ears:

how he'd had a wish. Look, we all have wishes; granted.
But who has wishes granted? Him. Do you know about
    gold?
It feeds no one; aurum, soft, untarnishable; slakes
no thirst. He tried to light a cigarette; I gazed, entranced,
as the blue flame played on its luteous stem. At least,
I said, you'll be able to give up smoking for good.

Separate beds. In fact, I put a chair against my door,
near petrified. He was below, turning the spare room
into the tomb of Tutankhamun. You see, we were
    passionate then,
in those halcyon days; unwrapping each other, rapidly,
like presents, fast food. But now I feared his honeyed
    embrace,
the kiss that would turn my lips to a work of art.

And who, when it comes to the crunch, can live
with a heart of gold? That night, I dreamt I bore
his child, its perfect ore limbs, its little tongue
like a precious latch, its amber eyes
holding their pupils like flies. My dream-milk
burned in my breasts. I woke to the streaming sun.

So he had to move out. We'd a caravan
in the wilds, in a glade of its own. I drove him up
under cover of dark. He sat in the back.
And then I came home, the woman who married the fool
who wished for gold. At first I visited, odd times,
parking the car a good way off, then walking.

You knew you were getting close. Golden trout
on the grass. One day, a hare hung from a larch,
a beautiful lemon mistake. And then his footprints,
glistening next to the river's path. He was thin,
delirious; hearing, he said, the music of Pan
from the woods. Listen. That was the last straw.

What gets me now is not the idiocy or greed
but lack of thought for me. Pure selfishness. I sold
the contents of the house and came down here.
I think of him in certain lights, dawn, late afternoon,
and once a bowl of apples stopped me dead. I miss most,
even now, his hands, his warm hands on my skin, his
   touch.

Mrs Aesop

By Christ, he could bore for Purgatory. He was small,
didn't prepossess. So he tried to impress. *Dead men,
Mrs Aesop*, he'd say, *tell no tales*. Well, let me tell you now
that the bird in his hand shat on his sleeve,
never mind the two worth less in the bush. Tedious.

Going out was worst. He'd stand at our gate, look, then leap;
scour the hedgerows for a shy mouse, the fields
for a sly fox, the sky for one particular swallow
that couldn't make a summer. The jackdaw, according to him,
envied the eagle. Donkeys would, on the whole, prefer to
    be lions.

On one appalling evening stroll, we passed an old hare
snoozing in a ditch – he stopped and made a note –
and then, about a mile further on, a tortoise, somebody's pet,
creeping, slow as marriage, up the road. *Slow
but certain, Mrs Aesop, wins the race*. Asshole.

What race? What sour grapes? What silk purse,
sow's ear, dog in a manger, what big fish? Some days,
I could barely keep awake as the story droned on
towards the moral of itself. *Action, Mrs A., speaks louder
than words*. And that's another thing, the sex

was diabolical. I gave him a fable one night
about a little cock that wouldn't crow, a razor-sharp axe
with a heart blacker than the pot that called the kettle.
I'll cut off your tail, all right, I said, *to save my face*.
That shut him up. I laughed last, longest.

Drunk

Suddenly the rain is hilarious.
The moon wobbles in the dusk.

What a laugh. Unseen frogs
belch in the damp grass.

The strange perfumes of darkening trees.
Cheap red wine

and the whole world a mouth.
Give me a double, a kiss.

Rounds

Eight pints
of lager, please,
and, of draught Guinness, nine;
two glasses of pale ale – a squeeze
of lemon in that port – a dry white wine,
four rums, three G-and-Ts, a vodka – that's the lot.
On second thoughts, you'd better give me one more double scotch.

A half
of scrumpy here
and, over there, a stout.
I think we're ready for more beer;
ten brandies, three martinis – no, my shout!
A triple advocaat with lemonade and lime
and six Bacardis – make that twelve, I've just noticed the time.

Six calves
of harlsberg – fast –
pine bitter shandies – tents –
and make the landies barge; a vast
treasure of mipple X, ten mème de crenthes,
nine muddy blaries and, of winger gine, a wealth.
Got that? And then the rame again all sound and one yourself.

Small Female Skull

With some surprise, I balance my small female skull in my
   hands.
What is it like? An ocarina? Blow in its eye.
It cannot cry, holds my breath only as long as I exhale,
mildly alarmed now, into the hole where the nose was,
press my ear to its grin. A vanishing sigh.

For some time, I sit on the lavatory seat with my head
in my hands, appalled. It feels much lighter than I'd thought;
the weight of a deck of cards, a slim volume of verse,
but with something else, as though it could levitate.
   Disturbing.
So why do I kiss it on the brow, my warm lips to its papery
   bone,

and take it to the mirror to ask for a gottle of geer?
I rinse it under the tap, watch dust run away, like sand
from a swimming-cap, then dry it – firstborn – gently
with a towel. I see the scar where I fell for sheer love
down treacherous stairs, and read that shattering day like
   braille.

Love, I murmur to my skull, then, louder, other grand words,
shouting the hollow nouns in a white-tiled room.
Downstairs they will think I have lost my mind. No. I
   only weep
into these two holes here, or I'm grinning back at the
   joke, this is
a friend of mine. See, I hold her face in trembling,
   passionate hands.

The Grammar of Light

Even barely enough light to find a mouth,
and bless both with a meaningless O, teaches,
spells out. The way a curtain opened at night
lets in neon, or moon, or a car's hasty glance,
and paints for a moment someone you love, pierces.

And so many mornings to learn; some
when the day is wrung from damp, grey skies
and rooms come on for breakfast
in the town you are leaving early. The way
a wasteground weeps glass tears at the end of a street.

Some fluent, showing you how the trees
in the square think in birds, telepathise. The way
the waiter balances light in his hands, the coins
in his pocket silver, and a young bell shines
in its white tower ready to tell.

Even a saucer of rain in a garden at evening
speaks to the eye. Like the little fires
from allotments, undressing in veils of mauve smoke
as you walk home under the muted lamps,
perplexed. The way the shy stars go stuttering on.

And at midnight, a candle next to the wine
slurs its soft wax, flatters. Shadows
circle the table. The way all faces blur
to dreams of themselves held in the eyes.
The flare of another match. The way everything dies.

Miles Away

I want you and you are not here. I pause
in this garden, breathing the colour thought is
before language into still air. Even your name
is a pale ghost and, though I exhale it again
and again, it will not stay with me. Tonight
I make you up, imagine you, your movements clearer
than the words I have you say you said before.

Wherever you are now, inside my head you fix me
with a look, standing here whilst cool late light
dissolves into the earth. I have got your mouth wrong,
but still it smiles. I hold you closer, miles away,
inventing love, until the calls of nightjars
interrupt and turn what was to come, was certain,
into memory. The stars are filming us for no one.

Adultery

Wear dark glasses in the rain.
Regard what was unhurt
as though through a bruise.
Guilt. A sick, green tint.

New gloves, money tucked in the palms,
the handshake crackles. Hands
can do many things. Phone.
Open the wine. Wash themselves. Now

you are naked under your clothes all day,
slim with deceit. Only the once
brings you alone to your knees,
miming, more, more, older and sadder,

creative. Suck a lie with a hole in it
on the way home from a lethal, thrilling night
up against a wall, faster. Language
unpeels to a lost cry. You're a bastard.

Do it do it do it. Sweet darkness
in the afternoon; a voice in your ear
telling you how you are wanted,
which way, now. A telltale clock

wiping the hours from its face, your face
on a white sheet, gasping, radiant, yes.
Pay for it in cash, fiction, cab-fares back
to the life which crumbles like a wedding-cake.

Paranoia for lunch; too much
to drink, as a hand on your thigh
tilts the restaurant. You know all about love,
don't you. Turn on your beautiful eyes

for a stranger who's dynamite in bed, again
and again; a slow replay in the kitchen
where the slicing of innocent onions
scalds you to tears. Then, selfish autobiographical sleep

in a marital bed, the tarnished spoon of your body
stirring betrayal, your heart over-ripe at the core.
You're an expert, darling; your flowers
dumb and explicit on nobody's birthday.

So write the script – illness and debt,
a ring thrown away in a garden
no moon can heal, your own words
commuting to bile in your mouth, terror –

and all for the same thing twice. And all
for the same thing twice. You did it.
What. Didn't you. Fuck. Fuck. No. That was
the wrong verb. This is only an abstract noun.

Alphabet for Auden

When the words have gone away
there is nothing left to say.

Unformed thought can never be,
what you feel is what you see,
write it down and set it free
on printed pages, © Me.
I love, you love, so does he –
long live English Poetry.
Four o'clock is time for tea,
I'll be Mother, who'll be me?

Murmur, underneath your breath,
incantations to the deaf.

Here we go again. Goody.
Art can't alter History.

Praise the language, treasure each
well-earned phrase your labours reach.

In hotels you sit and sigh,
crafting lines where others cry,

puzzled why it doesn't pay
shoving couplets round all day.
There is vodka on a tray.
Up your nose the hairs are grey.

When the words done gone it's hell
having nothing left to tell.

Pummel, punch, fondle, knead them
back again to life. Read them

when you doubt yourself and when
you doubt their function, read again.

Verse can say *I told you so*
but cannot sway the status quo

one inch. Now you get lonely,
Baby want love and love only.

In the mirror you see you.
Love you always, darling. True.

When the words have wandered far
poets patronise the bar,

understanding less and less.
Truth is anybody's guess

and Time's a clock, five of three,
mix another G-and-T.

Set 'em up, Joe, make that two.
Wallace Stevens thought in blue.

Words drown in a drunken sea,
dumb, they clutch at memory.

Pissed you have a double view,
something else to trouble you.

Inspiration clears the decks –
if all else fails, write of sex.

Every other word's a lie,
ain't no rainbow in the sky.

Some get lucky, die in bed,
one word stubbed in the ashtray. *Dead.*

Vicki Feaver

Slow Reader

He can make sculptures
and fabulous machines,
invent games, tell jokes,
give solemn, adult advice –
but he is slow to read.
When I take him on my knee
with his *Ladybird* book
he gazes into the air,
sighing and shaking his head
like an old man
who knows the mountains
are impassable.

He toys with words,
letting them go cold
as gristly meat,
until I relent
and let him wriggle free:
a fish returning
to its element,
or a white-eyed colt – shying
from the bit – who sees
that if he takes it
in his mouth
he'll never run
quite free again.

Mr Sparke

I

It was the worst winter in memory
his neighbour tells us, smoothing out
a cutting from the *Hexham Courant* —
a picture of already yellowing whiteness —
as if she thinks we don't believe her.

But we can see for ourselves: the grass
has hardly grown, spring flowers are late
coming through, and in a dip behind the far wood
there's a swathe of hard grey snow
with pine needles frozen in like splinters.

Up at Allenheads, she says, a man
who'd lived there all his life
and must have known the dangers
left his car and was buried in a drift.
They thought he'd have to have his hand off.

She'd been worried Mrs Sparke
would wander out again and be lost.
That's why she called the doctor.
Her husband dug a tunnel to the phone box —
it was like standing in an igloo.

The snow was piled so high
they had to climb on chairs to watch
for the ambulance from the window.
And after that they were cut off for weeks;
he never saw her again.

Mr Sparke's garden is as trim as ever.
The narrow borders by the path
are lined with scarlet tulips;
the soil is freshly dug and raked
ready for potatoes and the first seeds.

Dressed in his dark blue Sunday suit,
he calls to us, not to sit with him
in gloomy sympathy but to admire –
flanked by two china shepherdesses –
his new cassette recorder.

While he twists the silver buttons,
we wait uncomfortably, exchanging looks,
remembering those bulging watery eyes,
her matted unwashed hair,
the conversations leading nowhere.

He'd never seemed to notice she was ill.
He just kept on at that wall –
covering the stones with cement;
drawing the shapes of stones
on the smooth surface.

We try to think of an excuse to go.
But suddenly like ice melting in a thaw
the sound begins to flow –
an accordion band squeezing out
'What a friend we have in Jesus'.

And Mr Sparke is crying; rubbing
at his eyes with a work-swollen hand.
'What I always say is,' he shouts
above the noise, 'it's my belief
that time's a great healer.'

Marigolds

Not the flowers men give women –
delicately scented freesias,
stiff red roses, carnations
the shades of bridesmaids' dresses,
almost sapless flowers,
drying and fading – but flowers
that wilt as soon as their stems
are cut, leaves blackening
as if blighted by the enzymes
in our breath, rotting to a slime
we have to scour from the rims
of vases; flowers that burst
from tight, explosive buds, rayed
like the sun, that lit the path
up the Thracian mountain, that we wound
into our hair, stamped on
in ecstatic dance, that remind us
we are killers, can tear the heads
off men's shoulders;
flowers we still bring
secretly and shamefully
into the house, stroking
our arms and breasts and legs
with their hot orange fringes,
the smell of arousal.

Circe

Because he wouldn't enter me
I made her unenterable – Scylla,
the nymph who fled from the god
whose spawn and thrashing fish tail
I wanted. I spilled my powders
into the pool where she waded
to cool herself in the gauzy
noon heat – stayed to see her crotch
grow teeth, to watch her run
from her own legs.

My father is the fiery sun.
Why do I fall for cold men?
Picus, so beautiful
on his lathered horse
I couldn't move for burning.
I covered the moon, the stars,
even my father's furnace face
with the wet sponges of clouds,
conjured a boar from the air
for him to hunt, caught up with him
in a thicket, both of us gasping.
I thought he'd lick the sweat
from my small brown breasts
like the men in Venus's stories.
When I saw he was ready for flight
I gave him feathers.

I frighten men. Even Ulysses
I had to bargain with: a year in my bed
to set his friends upright again,
unglue their trotters.
I stretched nights into weeks –
lived in the damp, ripe, gooseberry rot
of my sheets, feeding my wanderer warrior
on jellies and syrups
to help him keep up with a goddess.
In the end, it was me who sent him away.
It made me too sad: hearing
my name on his tongue
like the hiss of a tide withdrawing.

Beauty and the Beast

He'd eat her eventually,
when he got tired
of watching her eat:

tucking the white napkin
into the top of her blouse,
picking the flesh

off a peacock's leg
with delicate teeth,
or with her tongue

sucking a clam
from its saucer shell.
After a few nights

he couldn't face
trotting to the fields
to pounce on a sheep.

While the pearl buttons
flew off her dresses,
his belly drooped

like an empty bag,
his fangs hung loose
in shrinking gums.

He sent her home to her father.
He knew he'd die
if he didn't eat raw meat.

On the day she came back
he lay in the long grass
of the rose garden,

eyes closed, meaning
to feast on her liver.
He heard her step, tasted

something wet and salt
on his lips, sensed hands
unzipping his furry pelt.

Wood-pigeons

The army chap says –
to get conversation flowing –
'Women are more adapted to life
than men. They get less hurt.
Keep more of themselves back.'

His wife of thirty years,
a bony, brainy woman
with pale, frizzy curls and
baby-blue eyes, gently remonstrates.
The others join in –

chuckling, smoothing,
while trying to wrestle
with small tough parcels
that sit in red pools of sauce
on each blue-patterned plate.

In the end, the hostess
has to raid the kitchen drawer
for the sharpest knives
so her guests can dismember
the wood-pigeons.

In her silver-beaded dress
she looks like the knife-thrower's girl
at the circus – carvers
bunched in her hands
like dangerous flowers.

Naked Girl with Egg

After Lucian Freud

While she discards coat, skirt,
cashmere sweater, a string of pearls,
and lies ready on the bed, left hand
propping her left breast, body twisted
in an S, he fries two eggs

and brings them in on a white dish.
Then he sets to work – his brush
slithering over lustrous flesh,
the coarse dark hair between her legs,
like a tongue seeking salt.

She keeps her mind fixed on the eggs,
as if by concentrating hard enough
she'll discover a meaning as obvious
as in one of those paintings
where a skull, bottom left, equals death.

What could be homelier, or more comforting,
than to dip toast soldiers
into soft yellow yolks? Yet she thinks
of a day on the moors when she trod
on a curlew's nest, and of herself

posed on the black coverlet
to satisfy something – still loose
in the world – that likes nothing better
than to be fed on a naked girl
with two fried eggs.

Oi Yoi Yoi

For Roger Hilton

The lady has no shame.
Wearing not a stitch
she is lolloping across
an abstract beach
towards a notional sea.

I like the whisker of hair
under her armpit. It suggests
that she's not one of those women
who are always trying to get rid
of their smell.

You were more interested
in her swinging baroque tits
and the space between her thighs
than the expression on her face.
That you've left blank.

But her *mons veneris*
you've etched in black ink
with the exuberance of a young lad
caught short on a bellyful of beer
scrawling on a wall in the Gents.

As a woman I ought to object.
But she looks happy enough.
And which of us doesn't occasionally
want one of the old gods to come down
and chase us over the sands?

The River God

doesn't know why he's such a strong swimmer;
why he drinks nothing but frothy black Guinness;
why when he stands at the top
of a long flight of stairs
he has to struggle to stop himself
raising his arms, diving into a pool
of swaying air; why in his fantasies
the girls undress – uncovering white necks
and shoulders, brown and pink-nippled breasts,
the dark nests between their legs –
among reeds, under the grey-yellow light
of willows; why the women – in bars,
airports, at the Tennis and Squash Club –
he never spends more than a night with
seem flaky, juiceless; why he wants to smear
their mouths and ears and stomachs
with slime; why the water he shakes
from his hair, that twists
off his shoulders in the shower,
glitters with sticklebacks, snails,
minnows; why his wife follows
his wet footprints with a cloth;
makes him wear slippers.

Ironing

I used to iron everything:
my iron flying over sheets and towels
like a sledge chased by wolves over snow,

the flex twisting and crinking
until the sheath frayed, exposing
wires like nerves. I stood like a horse

with a smoking hoof
inviting anyone who dared
to lie on my silver-padded board,

to be pressed to the thinness
of dolls cut from paper.
I'd have commandeered a crane

if I could, got the welders at Jarrow
to heat me an iron the size of a tug
to flatten the house.

Then for years I ironed nothing.
I put the iron in a high cupboard.
I converted to crumpledness.

And now I iron again: shaking
dark spots of water onto wrinkled
silk, nosing into sleeves, round

buttons, breathing the sweet heated smell
hot metal draws from newly washed
cloth, until my blouse dries

to a shining, creaseless blue,
an airy shape with room to push
my arms, breasts, lungs, heart into.

The Handless Maiden*

When all the water had run from her mouth,
and I'd rubbed her arms and legs,
and chest and belly and back,
with clumps of dried moss;
and I'd put her to sleep in a nest of grass,
and spread her dripping clothes on a bush,
and held her again – her heat passing
into my breast and shoulder,
the breath I couldn't believe in
like a tickling feather on my neck,
I let myself cry. I cried for my hands
my father cut off; for the lumpy, itching scars
of my stumps; for the silver hands –
my husband gave me – that spun and wove
but had no feeling; and for my handless arms
that let my baby drop – unwinding
from the tight swaddling cloth
as I drank from the brimming river.
And I cried for my hands that sprouted
in the red-orange mud – the hands
that write this, grasping
her curled fists.

*In Grimm's version of this story the woman's hands grow back
because she's good for seven years. But in a Russian version they
grow as she plunges her arms into a river to save her drowning
baby.

Crab Apple Jelly

Every year you said it wasn't worth the trouble –
you'd better things to do with your time –
and it made you furious when the jars
were sold at the church fête
for less than the cost of the sugar.

And every year you drove into the lanes
around Calverton to search
for the wild trees whose apples
looked as red and as sweet as cherries,
and tasted sourer than gooseberries.

You cooked them in the wide copper pan
Grandma brought with her from Wigan,
smashing them against the sides
with a long wooden spoon to split
the skins, straining the pulp

through an old muslin nappy.
It hung for days, tied with string
to the kitchen steps, dripping
into a bowl on the floor –
brown-stained, horrible,

a head in a bag, a pouch
of sourness, of all that went wrong
in that house of women. The last drops
you wrung out with your hands;
then, closing doors and windows

to shut out the clamouring wasps,
you boiled up the juice with sugar,
dribbling the syrup onto a cold plate
until it set to a glaze,
filling the heated jars.

When the jars were cool
you held one up to the light
to see if the jelly had cleared.
Oh Mummy, it was as clear and shining
as stained glass and the colour of fire.

The Singing Teacher

'Some girls' voices,' she said
through tight vermilion lips,
'come out like strings of sausages –
yours will have to be worked for.'
I looked down on hennaed hair,
child-size built-up shoes.
Something had gone wrong with her spine
to curl her back like a shrimp's.
I baked her cakes,
brought her bunches of flowers.
Aa-eh-ii-oh-oo, I sang,
while her fat white dog
trembled and whimpered in its dream
and she pinched me with pointed nails.
Oh, Miss Cree, forgive me
for what twisted through you
like a corkscrew: my budding
and growing, my nipples
that stood out like press-studs.

Women's Blood

Burn the soiled ones in the boiler,
my mother told me, showing me how to hook
the loops of gauze-covered wadding pads
onto an elastic belt, remembering
how my grandmother had given her
strips of rag she'd had to wash out
every month for herself: the grandmother
who had her chair by the boiler,
who I loved but was plotting to murder
before she murdered my mother, or my mother –
shaking, sobbing, hurling plates and cups,
screaming she wished she'd never been born,
screeching 'Devil!' and 'Witch!' –
murdered her. I piled up the pads
until the smell satisfied me
it was the smell of a corpse.
'How could you do such a thing?'
my mother asked, finding them
at the bottom of the wardrobe
where the year before she'd found
a cache of navy-blue knickers
stained with the black jelly clots
I thought were my wickedness
oozing out of me.

Rope

I gripped with my feet, climbed
until I could see through the hoops
of the netball posts; slid back –
burning the skin off my fingers.
Under the mound of coarse new hair,
curved bone, secretly folded flesh,
where the rope pressed, I'd roused
a live nest: a wriggling litter
like the baby voles I'd found
in a squeaking hole in the grass –
hearts palpitating in furless,
pastry-thin sides; or featherless
chicks – all claws and beaks
and black-veined wings –
that dropped from gutters.
I had to squeeze my thighs
to stop them breaking out –
squealing and squawking
into the gym's blue steel rafters,
or scrabbling down the inside
of my legs, over whitened plimsolls,
making the games mistress shriek.

Wasps

If you don't hurt them
they won't hurt you,
my father told me.

But I didn't believe him,
or that he wasn't afraid
as he wafted them

wildly away
with shaking,
nail-bitten fingers.

And now the wasps
have invaded again,
building a nest

in the roof-space,
scratching at the eaves
with fierce little jaws,

finding a way into rooms
through closed doors
and windows,

as they did in that other
heat-struck autumn
when we had to lift him

to change the sheets,
or rub surgical spirit
into his heels

and buttocks;
when a dozy wasp
crawled in

under his pyjama top
and clung like a brooch
to his bubbling chest.

Right Hand

Ever since, in an act of reckless
middle age, I broke my wrist
learning to skate, my right hand

refuses to sleep with me.
It performs the day's tasks
stiffly, stoically; but at night

slides out from the duvet
to hollow a nest in the pillow
like an animal gone to ground

in a hole in the hedge
whose instinct says have nothing
to do with heart, lungs, legs,

the dangerous head. I dreamed of gliding
through a Bruegel winter;
of sitting in smoky inns

drinking burning geneva.
My hand dreams its own dream
of escaping: a waving weed rooted

in a pool so icy and numbing
I can feel its ache
rising up my arm.

At Roisin's

We sit in her backyard under a Tree of Heaven,
water trickling round our feet.
She's left the hose running into the pond –
next door are pulling down a wall
and she doesn't want dust to choke the fish.

It was a miracle they survived the winter.
Every morning she had to come out
with buckets of hot water
to melt a hole in the ice
and free them from the frozen weed.

'Let me refresh your glass,' she says,
refilling it to the brim with gin
before I have a chance to protest
and leading me across the crazy paving
to watch the joyously leaping fish.

I used to come here a lot.
It cheered me up – the booze
and her telling me what a fool Bill was
(that I should have smashed a large
irreplaceable vase over his head)

and once a fantastic story
about a woman friend of hers
who hired a private plane
to drop leaflets printed YOU BITCH!
over her husband's mistress's house.

When I got home I'd doze
drunkenly on the sofa,
the children prodding me every so often
as if I was a fish under ice,
testing to see if I was still alive.

Climbing Tintagel

Ghosts don't exist,
you said, except as legends
in our head. But if they did
and we could choose
a haunting place

we wouldn't moon about
in graveyards, or return
to clank around our enemies;
we'd go back to where we once
were happiest: following

Arthur and his queen
up cliff and crag, no longer
stopping to catch breath,
or having to tread carefully
where the path crumbles

and our gaze drops
like a dislodged flint
three hundred feet
to black rocks
and leaping sea;

but leaving loosestrife,
primrose, violet,
untrampled, skimming gorse
and blackthorn hedge –
dancing out over the edge.

STC

For his biographer

First there are the jokes
about how it's going
on the 'South Col'
or the 'Big Sea';
but half-serious,

as if you really had returned
from inching your way
up a vertical rockface,
or sailing single-handed
across his painted ocean.

Then I ask about them –
those friends of yours
I've never met, but you
are now so intimate with
you know the day-to-day state

of souls and bowels.
Is Asra still keeping Sam
on a string? Did he really
see her in bed with William?
How are dear Dorothy's scarlet runners?

I suppose I'm jealous –
as a mountaineer's wife
is jealous of mountains,
or a lone sailor's
of the tug of the sea.

We sit in the Dawn of the Raj
after three days apart,
sharing a Tandoori Mixed Grill,
discussing our passions
and our problems

and you have that far-away look
as if it's all going on
in another room
on another floor
of another century.

The Crack

cut right through the house:
a thick wiggly line
you could poke a finger into,
a deep gash seeping
fine black dust.

It didn't appear overnight.
For a long time
it was such a fine line
we went up and down stairs
oblivious to the stresses

that were splitting
our walls and ceilings apart.
And even when it thickened
and darkened, we went on
not seeing, or seeing

but believing the crack
would heal itself,
if dry earth was to blame,
a winter of rain
would seal its edges.

You didn't tell me
that you heard at night
its faint stirrings
like something alive.
And I didn't tell you –

until the crack
had opened so wide
that if we'd moved in our sleep
to reach for each other
we'd have fallen through.

Lily Pond

Thinking of new ways to kill you
and bring you back from the dead,
I try drowning you in the lily pond –

holding your head down
until every bubble of breath
is squeezed from your lungs

and the flat leaves and spiky flowers
float over you like a wreath.
I sit on the stones until I'm numb,

until, among reflections of sky,
water-buttercups, spears of iris,
your face rises to the surface –

a face that was always puffy
and pale, so curiously unchanged.
A wind rocks the waxy flowers, curls

the edges of the leaves. Blue dragonflies
appear and vanish like ghosts.
I part the mats of yellow weed

and drag you to the bank, covering
your green algae-stained corpse
with a white sheet. Then, I lift the edge

and climb in underneath –
thumping your chest,
breathing into your mouth.

White Tulips

Last night I saw you in my dream:
wrenching the hands off clocks,
tearing out springs, weights, jewels.
And now I find you in an orchard,
lying face-up under red blossom
like one of those stone kings
with lion cubs at their feet.
There's a smile on your face;
you're surrounded by white tulips.
You must have cored the earth,
pushed home the papery bulbs
just for this moment – knowing
I'd peer through locked gates,
pressing my forehead against
a blacksmith's tracery
of bells and whorled leaves.
I feel myself shrinking, drying –
skin, bones, nerves, veins
contracting. I fly into the white bowls
of the flowers, emerge sticky with nectar
and pollen, alight on your neck, crawl
under your shirt, and sting.

Bitch Swimming

You were the one who acted dog:
imprinting me with a smell
stronger than distance,
disaffection; nose and tongue,
and teeth I could never be sure
were playful, centred on rump
and neck; exciting a bitch
in me, who, while I rehearse
reasons why I'm better off
without you, has leapt
over the wall of a garden,
is in at a door, snuffling
up stairs, pushing her slender
delicate nose into a bed,
whimpering, howling,
tugging at sticky,
stained sheets.
     There's only one way
to lose a scent. I jump into a pool
of unknown depth: surface
among midges, bubbles,
floating feathers –
make us swim for our lives.

Judith

Wondering how a good woman can murder
I enter the tent of Holofernes,
holding in one hand his long oiled hair
and in the other, raised above
his sleeping, wine-flushed face,
his falchion with its unsheathed
curved blade. And I feel a rush
of tenderness, a longing
to put down my weapon, to lie
sheltered and safe in a warrior's
fumy sweat, under the emerald stars
of his purple and gold canopy,
to melt like a sweet on his tongue
to nothing. And I remember the glare
of the barley field; my husband
pushing away the sponge I pressed
to his burning head; the stubble
puncturing my feet as I ran,
flinging myself on a body
that was already cooling
and stiffening; and the nights
when I lay on the roof – my emptiness
like the emptiness of a temple
with the doors kicked in; and the mornings
when I rolled in the ash of the fire
just to be touched and dirtied
by something. And I bring my blade

down on his neck — and it's easy
like slicing through fish.
And I bring it down again,
cleaving the bone.

Lacrimae Hominis

You've cried three times, you say:
once when your mother died,
once when you visited her grave,
and now, in powdery dawn,
as I sing, tentatively,
a song she used to sing,
'The Ballad of Barbara Allen'.
Are you crying? Your eyes shine –
but the cheeks I touch
are hot, waterless.
If I dived into the black light
of your pupils, I'd break my head
in a dry pool. If I took an axe to you,
you'd weep like a fir –
resinous tears, amber drops
hardening in the air.

Li Ho

is bounding through the forest
with a big smile on his face.
Fruits fall into his hands

from the overhanging branches,
fish leap from streams at his feet.
He thinks he's in paradise.

It's the first day of his holidays.
He's said farewell to his honourable masters,
drained out the tinkling waterclock,

and now he's going to sail his boat
on the lake and write the poems
that all winter have been nibbling

at the lines in his head. But first
he's promised himself he'll mend an old box
with a picture on the lid

cut intricately in jade
of a man bounding through a forest
with a big smile on his face

who keeps a box on his desk
with nothing inside it
to prove that space exists.

Voyage

So at last I set a course
for the rough water
beyond the bay;

and all night long –
green and groaning –
I sailed away.

And now, on this calm morning,
I look down into a glassy harbour
where gold- and silver-striped

words are darting,
and the gap-mouthed dead
are floating

and where the flotsam
is so familiar –
things once in my possession

washed there
by a solicitous ocean
to make the landfall welcoming.

Bufo Bufo

Clown's name for the creature
in my cellar. I give him gladly

the one room I don't want –
sodden cardboard, wet dark,

the gluey varnish of slugs.
What he eats: dollops

of glassy, yellow-grey meat,
host to scavenging mites,

the only things down here
to move fast. He creeps

over the floor's uneven brick
as if movement is painful,

or crouches still, under the drip
from a leaking pipe, moist

and glistening, pumping
himself to bursting.

It's spring, when toads smell their way
to water, and the females' spawn

is strung in necklaces of black-eyed beads.
But he's my prisoner – soft, warty stone

who at night swells
to the size of a man.

Horned Poppy

Frailest of flowers, armoured to survive
at the edge of the sea: leaves
tough like holly, hugging the stem
like spiked cuffs; the bud protected
by a prickly sheath; the petals furled
like yellow parachute silk, opening to expose,
at its radiant heart, the threads
of stamens, pollen's loose dust.
It blooms for at the most an hour;
torn apart by the elements it loves.
And then the pistil grows:
a live bootlace, a fuse
of multiplying cells – reaching out
to feel between the shingle's
sharp-edged flints for a moist bed
to lay its seed; or in my kitchen,
drying in the heat, a long thin hand
summoning a salt gale, a tide to roll in
over the flat land, roaring
through the open door.

The Red Cupboard

After Pierre Bonnard

The woman's cupboard, she's stocked
with jams, jellies, pickled limes

and bottles of blue-skinned plums
that just to look at is to taste

their sweet green flesh. Inset in the wall,
the inside's painted the red of petals –

poppies, geraniums – of dream blood.
When she opens the white door

it's like opening herself.
Among jars of quince and apple,

the red satin dress with a boned bodice
she wore as a girl; and multiplied behind,

down a long corridor of deepening reds,
the woman who each month either swelled

with a child, or felt the little burp
and bubble that began her flow.

And beyond, in black red fields,
her mother, and her grandmother,

and her grandmother's mother –
a queue stretching back, back.

Some days, when she opens the door
on her riches, her gifts, her sumptuous store,

all that's left
is the thick scent of blood.

Glow Worm

Talking about the chemical changes
that make a body in love shine,
or even, for months, immune to illness,
you pick a grub from the lawn
and let it lie on your palm – glowing
like the emerald-burning butt
of a cigarette. (We still haven't touched,
only lain side by side
the half stories of our half lives.)
You call them lightning bugs
from the way the males gather in clouds
and simultaneously flash.
This is the female, fat from a diet
of liquefied snails, at the stage in her cycle
when she hardly eats; when all her energy's
directed to drawing water and oxygen
to a layer of luciferin.
Wingless, wordless,
in a flagrant and luminous bid
to resist the narrative's pull to death,
she lifts her shining green abdomen
to signal *yes yes yes*.

Eavan Boland

The War Horse

This dry night, nothing unusual
About the clip, clop, casual

Iron of his shoes as he stamps death
Like a mint on the innocent coinage of earth.

I lift the window, watch the ambling feather
Of hock and fetlock, loosed from its daily tether

In the tinker camp on the Enniskerry Road,
Pass, his breath hissing, his snuffling head

Down. He is gone. No great harm is done.
Only a leaf of our laurel hedge is torn –

Of distant interest like a maimed limb,
Only a rose which now will never climb

The stone of our house, expendable, a mere
Line of defence against him, a volunteer

You might say, only a crocus its bulbous head
Blown from growth, one of the screamless dead.

But we, we are safe, our unformed fear
Of fierce commitment gone; why should we care

If a rose, a hedge, a crocus are uprooted
Like corpses, remote, crushed, mutilated?

He stumbles on like a rumour of war, huge,
Threatening; neighbours use the subterfuge

Of curtains; he stumbles down our short street
Thankfully passing us. I pause, wait.

Then to breathe relief lean on the sill
And for a second only my blood is still

With atavism. That rose he smashed frays
Ribboned across our hedge, recalling days

Of burned countryside, illicit braid:
A cause ruined before, a world betrayed.

Child of Our Time

For Aengus

Yesterday I knew no lullaby
But you have taught me overnight to order
This song, which takes from your final cry
Its tune, from your unreasoned end its reason;
Its rhythm from the discord of your murder,
Its motive from the fact you cannot listen.

We who should have known how to instruct,
With rhymes for your waking, rhythms for your sleep,
Names for the animals you took to bed,
Tales to distract, legends to protect,
Later an idiom for you to keep
And living, learn, must learn from you, dead,

To make our broken images rebuild
Themselves around your limbs, your broken
Image, find for your sake whose life our idle
Talk has cost, a new language. Child
Of our time, our times have robbed your cradle.
Sleep in a world your final sleep has woken.

17 May 1974
(on the occasion of a baby killed in the Dublin bombing)

Mise Eire

I won't go back to it –

my nation displaced
into old dactyls,
oaths made
by the animal tallows
of the candle –

land of the Gulf Stream,
the small farm,
the scalded memory,
the songs
that bandage up the history,
the words
that make a rhythm of the crime

where time is time past.
A palsy of regrets.
No. I won't go back.
My roots are brutal:

I am the woman –
a sloven's mix
of silk at the wrists,
a sort of dove-strut
in the precincts of the garrison –

who practises
the quick frictions,
the rictus of delight
and gets cambric for it,
rice-coloured silks.

I am the woman
in the gansy-coat
on board the *Mary Belle*,
in the huddling cold,

holding her half-dead baby to her
as the wind shifts east
and north over the dirty
water of the wharf

mingling the immigrant
guttural with the vowels
of homesickness who neither
knows nor cares that

a new language
is a kind of scar
and heals after a while
into a passable imitation
of what went before.

The Oral Tradition

I was standing there
at the end of a reading
or a workshop or whatever,
watching people heading
out into the weather,

only half-wondering
what becomes of words,
the brisk herbs of language,
the fragrances we think we sing,
if anything.

We were left behind
in a firelit room
in which the colour scheme
crouched well down –
golds, a sort of dun

a distressed ochre –
and the sole richness was
in the suggestion of a texture
like the low flax gleam
that comes off polished leather.

Two women
were standing in shadow,
one with her back turned.
Their talk was a gesture,
an outstretched hand.

They talked to each other,
and words like 'summer',
'birth', 'great-grandmother'
kept pleading with me,
urging me to follow.

'She could feel it coming' –
one of them was saying –
'all the way there,
across the fields at evening
and no one there, God help her

'and she had on a skirt
of cross-woven linen
and the little one
kept pulling at it.
It was nearly night . . .'

(Wood hissed and split
in the open grate,
broke apart in sparks,
a windfall of light
in the room's darkness)

'. . . when she lay down
and gave birth to him
in an open meadow.
What a child that was
to be born without a blemish!'

It had started raining,
the windows dripping, misted.
One moment I was standing
not seeing out,
only half-listening

staring at the night; the next
without warning
I was caught by it:
the bruised summer light,
the musical subtext

of mauve eaves on lilac
and the laburnum past
and shadows where the lime
tree dropped its bracts
in frills of contrast

where she lay down
in vetch and linen
and lifted up her son
to the archive
they would shelter in:

the oral song
avid as superstition,
layered like an amber in
the wreck of language
and the remnants of a nation.

I was getting out
my coat, buttoning it,
shrugging up the collar.
It was bitter outside,
a real winter's night

and I had distances
ahead of me: iron miles
in trains, iron rails
repeating instances
and reasons; the wheels

singing innuendoes, hints,
outlines underneath
the surface, a sense
suddenly of truth,
its resonance.

Night Feed

This is dawn.
Believe me
This is your season, little daughter.
The moment daisies open,
The hour mercurial rainwater
Makes a mirror for sparrows.
It's time we drowned our sorrows.

I tiptoe in.
I lift you up
Wriggling
In your rosy, zipped sleeper.
Yes, this is the hour
For the early bird and me
When finder is keeper.

I crook the bottle.
How you suckle!
This is the best I can be,
Housewife
To this nursery
Where you hold on,
Dear Life.

A silt of milk.
The last suck.
And now your eyes are open,
Birth-coloured and offended.
Earth wakes.
You go back to sleep.
The feed is ended.

Worms turn.
Stars go in.
Even the moon is losing face.
Poplars stilt for dawn
And we begin
The long fall from grace.
I tuck you in.

Domestic Interior

For Kevin

The woman is as round
as the new ring
ambering her finger.
The mirror weds her.
She has long since been bedded.

There is
about it all
a quiet search for attention,
like the unexpected shine
of a despised utensil.

The oils,
the varnishes,
the cracked light,
the worm of permanence –
all of them supplied by Van Eyck –

by whose edict she will stay
burnished, fertile
on her wedding day,
interred in her joy.
Love, turn.

The convex of your eye
that is so loving, bright
and constant yet shows
only this woman in her varnishes,
who won't improve in the light.

But there's a way of life
that is its own witness:
put the kettle on, shut the blind.
Home is a sleeping child,
an open mind

and our effects,
shrugged and settled
in the sort of light
jugs and kettles
grow important by.

Self-portrait on a Summer Evening

Jean-Baptiste Chardin
is painting a woman
in the last summer light.

All summer long
he has been slighting her
in botched blues, tints,
half-tones, rinsed neutrals.

What you are watching
is light unlearning itself,
an infinite unfrocking of the prism.

Before your eyes
the ordinary life
is being glazed over:
pigments of the bibelot,
the cabochon, the water-opal
pearl to the intimate
simple colours of
her ankle-length summer skirt.

Can't you feel it?
Aren't you chilled by it?
The way the late afternoon
is reduced to detail —

the sky that odd shade of apron —
opaque, scumbled —
the lazulis of the horizon becoming
optical greys
before your eyes
before your eyes
in my ankle-length
summer skirt

crossing between
the garden and the house,
under the whitebeam trees,
keeping an eye on
the length of the grass,
the height of the hedge,
the distance of the children

I am Chardin's woman

edged in reflected light,
hardened by
the need to be ordinary.

The Women

This is the hour I love: the in-between
neither here-nor-there hour of evening.
The air is tea-coloured in the garden.
The briar rose is spilled crêpe de Chine.

This is the time I do my work best,
going up the stairs in two minds,
in two worlds, carrying cloth or glass,
leaving something behind, bringing
something with me I should have left behind.

The hour of change, of metamorphosis,
of shape-shifting instabilities.
My time of sixth sense and second sight
when in the words I choose, the lines I write,
they rise like visions and appear to me:

women of work, of leisure, of the night,
in stove-coloured silks, in lace, in nothing,
with crewel needles, with books, with wide-open legs,

who fled the hot breath of the god pursuing,
who ran from the split hoof and the thick lips
and fell and grieved and healed into myth,

into me in the evening at my desk
testing the water with a sweet quartet,
the physical force of a dissonance –

the fission of music into syllabic heat –
and getting sick of it and standing up
and going downstairs in the last brightness

into a landscape without emphasis,
light, linear, precisely planned,
a hemisphere of tiered, aired cotton,

a hot terrain of linen from the iron,
folded in and over, stacked high,
neatened flat, stoving heat and white.

Lace

Bent over
the open notebook –

light fades out
making the trees stand out
and my room
at the back
of the house, dark.

In the dusk
I am still
looking for it –
the language that is

lace:

a baroque obligation
at the wrist
of a prince
in a petty court.
Look, just look
at the way he shakes out

the thriftless phrases
the crystal rhetoric
of bobbined knots
and bosses:
a vagrant drift
of emphasis

to wave away an argument
or frame the hand
he kisses;
which, for all that, is still

what someone
in the corner
of a room,
in the dusk,
bent over
as the light was failing

lost their sight for.

The Journey

For Elizabeth Ryle

Immediately cries were heard. These were the loud wailing of infant
souls at the very entranceway; never had they had their share of life's
sweetness for the dark day had stolen them from their mothers'
breasts and plunged them to a death before their time.

Virgil, *The Aeneid*, Book VI

And then the dark fell and 'there has never'
I said 'been a poem to an antibiotic:
never a word to compare with the odes on
the flower of the raw sloe for fever

'or the devious Africa-seeking tern
or the protein treasures of the sea bed.
Depend on it, somewhere a poet is wasting
his sweet uncluttered metres on the obvious

'emblem instead of the real thing.
Instead of sulpha we shall have hyssop dipped
in the wild blood of the unblemished lamb,
so every day the language gets less

'for the task and we are less with the language.'
I finished speaking and the anger faded
and dark fell and the book beside me
lay open at the page Aphrodite

comforts Sappho in her love's duress.
The poplars shifted their music in the garden,
a child startled in a dream,
my room was a mess –

the usual hardcovers, half-finished cups,
clothes piled up on an old chair –
and I was listening out but in my head was
a loosening and sweetening heaviness,

not sleep, but nearly sleep, not dreaming really
but as ready to believe and still
unfevered, calm and unsurprised
when she came and stood beside me

and I would have known her anywhere
and I would have gone with her anywhere
and she came wordlessly
and without a word I went with her

down down down without so much as
ever touching down but always, always
with a sense of mulch beneath us,
the way of stairs winding down to a river

and as we went on the light went on
failing and I looked sideways to be certain
it was she, misshapen, musical –
Sappho – the scholiast's nightingale

and down we went, again down
until we came to a sudden rest
beside a river in what seemed to be
an oppressive suburb of the dawn.

My eyes got slowly used to the bad light.
At first I saw shadows, only shadows.
Then I could make out women and children
and, in the way they were, the grace of love.

'Cholera, typhus, croup, diphtheria,'
she said, 'in those days they racketed
in every backstreet and alley of old Europe.
Behold the children of the plague.'

Then to my horror I could see to each
nipple some had clipped a limpet shape –
suckling darknesses – while others had their arms
weighed down, making terrible pietas.

She took my sleeve and said to me 'be careful.
Do not define these women by their work:
not as washerwomen trussed in dust and sweating,
muscling water into linen by the river's edge

'nor as court ladies brailled in silk
on wool, and woven with an ivory unicorn
and hung, nor as laundresses tossing cotton,
brisking daylight with lavender and gossip.

'But these are women who went out like you
when dusk became a dark sweet with leaves,
recovering the day, stooping, picking up
teddy bears and rag dolls and tricycles and buckets –

'love's archaeology – and they too like you
stood boot deep in flowers once in summer
or saw winter come in with a single magpie
in a caul of haws, a solo harlequin.'

I stood fixed. I could not reach or speak to them.
Between us was the melancholy river,
the dream water, the narcotic crossing.
They had passed over it, its cold persuasions.

I whispered, 'let me be
let me at least be their witness,' but she said
'what you have seen is beyond speech,
beyond song, only not beyond love;

'remember it, you will remember it'
and I heard her say but she was fading fast
as we emerged under the stars of heaven,
'there are not many of us; you are dear

'and stand beside me as my own daughter.
I have brought you here so you will know forever
the silences in which are our beginnings,
in which we have an origin like water,'

and the wind shifted and the window clasp
opened, banged and I woke up to find
my poetry books spread higgledy-piggledy,
my skirt spread out where I had laid it –

nothing was changed; nothing was more clear
but it was wet and the year was late.
The rain was grief in arrears; my children
slept the last dark out safely and I wept.

Envoi

It is Easter in the suburb. Clematis
shrubs the eaves and trellises with pastel.
The evenings lengthen and before the rain
the Dublin mountains become visible.

My muse must be better than those of men
who made theirs in the image of their myth.
The work is half-finished and I have nothing
but the crudest measures to complete it with.

Under the street lamps the dustbins brighten.
The winter-flowering jasmine casts a shadow
outside my window in my neighbour's garden.
These are the things that my muse must know.

She must come to me. Let her come
to be among the donnée, the given.
I need her to remain with me until
the day is over and the song is proven.

Surely she comes, surely she comes to me –
no lizard skin, no paps, no podded womb
about her but a brightening and
the consequences of an April tomb.

What I have done I have done alone.
What I have seen is unverified.
I have the truth and I need the faith.
It is time I put my hand in her side.

If she will not bless the ordinary,
if she will not sanctify the common,
then here I am and here I stay and then am I
the most miserable of women.

The Making of an Irish Goddess

Ceres went to hell
with no sense of time.

When she looked back
all that she could see was

the arteries of silver in the rock,
the diligence of rivers always at one level,
wheat at one height,
leaves of a single colour,
the same distance in the usual light;

a seasonless, unscarred earth.

But I need time –
my flesh and that history –
to make the same descent:

In my body,
neither young now nor fertile,
and with the marks of childbirth
still on it,

in my gestures –
the way I pin my hair to hide
the stitched, healed blemish of a scar –
must be

an accurate inscription
of that agony:

the failed harvests,
the fields rotting to the horizon,
the children devoured by their mothers
whose souls, they would have said,
went straight to hell,
followed by their own.

There is no other way:

Myth is the wound we leave
in the time we have –

which in my case is this
March evening
at the foothills of the Dublin mountains,
across which the lights have changed all day,

holding up my hand
sickle-shaped, to my eyes
to pick out
my own daughter from
all the other children in the distance;

her back turned to me.

The Emigrant Irish

Like oil lamps, we put them out the back –

of our houses, of our minds. We had lights
better than, newer than and then

a time came, this time and now
we need them. Their dread, makeshift example:

they would have thrived on our necessities.
What they survived we could not even live.
By their lights now it is time to
imagine how they stood there, what they stood with,
that their possessions may become our power:

Cardboard. Iron. Their hardships parcelled in them.
Patience. Fortitude. Long-suffering
in the bruise-coloured dusk of the New World.

And all the old songs. And nothing to lose.

Bright-cut Irish Silver

I take it down
from time to time, to feel
the smooth path of silver meet the cicatrix of skill.

These scars, I tell myself, are learned.

This gift for wounding an artery of rock
was passed on from father to son, to the father
of the next son.

Is an aptitude for injuring
earth while inferring it in curves and surfaces.

Is this cold potency which has come –
by time and chance –

into my hands.

The Achill Woman

She came up the hill carrying water.
She wore a half-buttoned, wool cardigan,
a tea-towel round her waist.

She pushed the hair out of her eyes with
her free hand and put the bucket down.

The zinc-music of the handle on the rim
tuned the evening. An Easter moon rose.
In the next-door field a stream was
a fluid sunset; and then, stars.

I remember the cold rosiness of her hands.
She bent down and blew on them like broth.
And round her waist, on a white background,
in coarse, woven letters, the words 'glass cloth'.

And she was nearly finished for the day.
And I was all talk, raw from college –
weekending at a friend's cottage
with one suitcase and the set text
of the Court poets of the Silver Age.

We stayed putting down time until
the evening turned cold without warning.
She said goodnight and started down the hill.

The grass changed from lavender to black.
The trees turned back to cold outlines.
You could taste frost

but nothing now can change the way I went
indoors, chilled by the wind

and made a fire
and took down my book
and opened it and failed to comprehend

the harmonies of servitude,
the grace music gives to flattery
and language borrows from ambition –

and how I fell asleep
oblivious to

the planets clouding over in the skies,
the slow decline of the spring moon,
the songs crying out their ironies.

An Old Steel Engraving

Look.
The figure in the foreground breaks his fall with
one hand. He cannot die.
The river cannot wander
into the shadows to be dragged by willows.
The passerby is scared witless. He cannot escape.
He cannot stop staring at
this hand which can barely raise
the patriot
above the ground which is
the origin and reason for it all.

More closely now:
at the stillness of unfinished action in
afternoon heat, at the spaces on the page. They widen
to include us:
we have found
the country of our malediction where
nothing can move until we find the word,
nothing can stir until we say this is
what happened and is happening and history
is one of us who turns away
while the other is
turning the page.

Is this river which
moments ago must have flashed the morse
of a bayonet thrust. And is moving on.

White Hawthorn in the West of Ireland

I drove west
in the season between seasons.
I left behind suburban gardens.
Lawnmowers. Small talk.

Under low skies, past splashes of coltsfoot
I assumed
the hard shyness of Atlantic light
and the superstitious aura of hawthorn.

All I wanted then was to fill my arms with
sharp flowers,
to seem, from a distance, to be part of
that ivory, downhill rush. But I knew,

I had always known
the custom was
not to touch hawthorn.
Not to bring it indoors for the sake of

the luck
such constraint would forfeit —
a child might die, perhaps, or an unexplained
fever speckle heifers. So I left it

stirring on those hills
with a fluency
only water has. And, like water, able
to redefine land. And free to seem to be —

for anglers,
and for travellers astray in
the unmarked lights of a May dusk —
the only language spoken in those parts.

Outside History

There are outsiders, always. These stars –
these iron inklings of an Irish January,
whose light happened

thousands of years before
our pain did: they are, they have always been
outside history.

They keep their distance. Under them remains
a place where you found
you were human, and

a landscape in which you know you are mortal.
And a time to choose between them.
I have chosen:

Out of myth into history I move to be
part of that ordeal
whose darkness is

only now reaching me from those fields,
those rivers, those roads clotted as
firmaments with the dead.

How slowly they die
as we kneel beside them, whisper in their ear.
And we are too late. We are always too late.

Distances

The radio is playing downstairs in the kitchen.
The clock says eight and the light says
winter. You are pulling up your hood against a bad morning.

Don't leave, I say. Don't go without telling me
the name of that song. You call it back to me from the stairs:
'I Wish I Was In Carrickfergus'

and the words open out with emigrant grief the way the streets
of a small town open out in
memory: salt-loving fuchsias to one side and

a market in full swing on the other with
linen for sale and tacky apples and a glass and wire hill
of spectacles on a metal tray. The front door bangs

and you're gone. I will think of it all morning while a fine
drizzle closes in, making the distances
fiction: not of that place but this and of how

restless we would be, you and I, inside the perfect
music of that basalt and sandstone
coastal town. We would walk the streets in

the scentless afternoon of a ballad measure,
longing to be able
to tell each other that the starched lace and linen of

adult handkerchiefs scraped your face and left your tears
falling; how the apples were mush inside the crisp sugar
shell and the spectacles out of focus.

The Black Lace Fan My Mother Gave Me

It was the first gift he ever gave her,
buying it for five francs in the Galeries
in prewar Paris. It was stifling.
A starless drought made the nights stormy.

They stayed in the city for the summer.
They met in cafés. She was always early.
He was late. That evening he was later.
They wrapped the fan. He looked at his watch.

She looked down the Boulevard des Capucines.
She ordered more coffee. She stood up.
The streets were emptying. The heat was killing.
She thought the distance smelled of rain and lightning.

These are wild roses, appliquéd on silk by hand,
darkly picked, stitched boldly, quickly.
The rest is tortoiseshell and has the reticent,
clear patience of its element. It is

a worn-out underwater bullion and it keeps,
even now, an inference of its violation.
The lace is overcast as if the weather
it opened for and offset had entered it.

The past is an empty café terrace.
An airless dusk before thunder. A man running.
And no way now to know what happened then –
none at all – unless, of course, you improvise:

the blackbird on this first sultry morning,
in summer, finding buds, worms, fruit,
feels the heat. Suddenly she puts out her wing –
the whole, full, flirtatious span of it.

The Parcel

There are dying arts and
one of them is
the way my mother used to make up a parcel.
Paper first. Mid-brown and coarse-grained as wood.
The worst sort for covering a Latin book neatly
or laying flat at Christmas on a pudding bowl.
It was a big cylinder. She snipped it open
and it unrolled quickly across the floor.
All business, all distance.
Then the scissors:
not a glittering let-up but a dour
pair, black thumb-holes,
the shears themselves the colour of the rained-
on steps a man with a grindstone climbed up
in the season of lilac and snapdragon
and stood there arguing the rate for
sharpening the lawnmower and the garden pair
and this one. All-in.
The ball of twine was coarsely braided
and only a shade less yellow than
the flame she held under the blunt
end of the sealing wax until
it melted and spread into a brittle
terracotta medal.
Her hair dishevelled, her tongue between her teeth,
she wrote the address in the quarters
twine had divided the surface into.
Names and places. Crayon and fountain pen.
The town underlined once. The country twice.

It's ready for the post
she would say and if we want to know
where it went to –
a craft lost before we missed it – watch it go
into the burlap sack for collection.
See it disappear. Say
this is how it died
out: among doomed steamships and outdated trains,
the tracks for them disappearing before our eyes,
next to station names we can't remember
on a continent we no longer
recognize. The sealing wax cracking.
The twine unravelling. The destination illegible.

That the Science of Cartography is Limited

– and not simply by the fact that this shading of
forest cannot show the fragrance of balsam,
the gloom of cypresses,
is what I wish to prove.

When you and I were first in love we drove
to the borders of Connacht
and entered a wood there.

Look down you said: this was once a famine road.

I looked down at ivy and the scutch grass
rough-cast stone had
disappeared into as you told me
in the second winter of their ordeal, in

1847, when the crop had failed twice,
Relief Committees gave
the starving Irish such roads to build.

Where they died, there the road ended

and ends still and when I take down
the map of this island, it is never so
I can say here is
the masterful, the apt rendering of

the spherical as flat, nor
an ingenious design which persuades a curve
into a plane,
but to tell myself again that

the line which says woodland and cries hunger
and gives out among sweet pine and cypress,
and finds no horizon

will not be there.

Beautiful Speech

In my last year in College
I set out
to write an essay on
the Art of Rhetoric. I had yet to find

the country already lost to me
in song and figure as I scribbled down
names for sweet euphony
and safe digression.

And when I came to the word *insinuate*
I saw that language could writhe and creep
and the lore of snakes
which I had learned as a child not to fear –
because the Saint had sent them out of Ireland –
came nearer.

Chiasmus. Litotes. Periphrasis. Old
indices and agents of persuasion. How
I remember them in that room where
a girl is writing at a desk with
dusk already in
the streets outside. I can see her. I could say to her –

we will live, we have lived
where language is concealed. Is perilous.
We will be – we have been – citizens
of its hiding place. But it is too late

to shut the book of satin phrases,
to refuse to enter
an evening bitter with peat smoke,
where newspaper sellers shout headlines
and friends call out their farewells in
a city of whispers
and interiors where

the dear vowels
Irish Ireland ours are
absorbed into Autumn air,
are out of earshot in the distances
we are stepping into where we never

imagine words such as *hate*
and *territory* and the like – unbanished still
as they always would be – wait
and are waiting under
beautiful speech. To strike.

This Moment

A neighbourhood.
At dusk.

Things are getting ready
to happen
out of sight.

Stars and moths.
And rinds slanting around fruit.

But not yet.

One tree is black.
One window is yellow as butter.

A woman leans down to catch a child
who has run into her arms
this moment.

Stars rise.
Moths flutter.
Apples sweeten in the dark.

Love

Dark falls on this mid-western town
where we once lived when myths collided.
Dusk has hidden the bridge in the river
which slides and deepens
to become the water
the hero crossed on his way to hell.

Not far from here is our old apartment.
We had a kitchen and an Amish table.
We had a view. And we discovered there
love had the feather and muscle of wings
and had come to live with us,
a brother of fire and air.

We had two infant children one of whom
was touched by death in this town
and spared: and when the hero
was hailed by his comrades in hell
their mouths opened and their voices failed and
there is no knowing what they would have asked
about a life they had shared and lost.

I am your wife.
It was years ago.
Our child is healed. We love each other still.
Across our day-to-day and ordinary distances
we speak plainly. We hear each other clearly.

And yet I want to return to you
on the bridge of the Iowa river as you were,
with snow on the shoulders of your coat
and a car passing with its headlights on:

I see you as a hero in a text –
the image blazing and the edges gilded –
and I long to cry out the epic question
my dear companion:
Will we ever live so intensely again?
Will love come to us again and be
so formidable at rest it offered us ascension
even to look at him?

But the words are shadows and you cannot hear me.
You walk away and I cannot follow.

The Pomegranate

The only legend I have ever loved is
The story of a daughter lost in hell.
And found and rescued there.
Love and blackmail are the gist of it.
Ceres and Persephone the names.
And the best thing about the legend is
I can enter it anywhere. And have.
As a child in exile in
A city of fogs and strange consonants,
I read it first and at first I was
An exiled child in the crackling dusk of
The underworld, the stars blighted. Later
I walked out in a summer twilight
Searching for my daughter at bedtime.
When she came running I was ready
To make any bargain to keep her.
I carried her back past whitebeams.
And wasps and honey-scented buddleias.
But I was Ceres then and I knew
Winter was in store for every leaf
On every tree on that road.
Was inescapable for each one we passed.
And for me.
It is winter
And the stars are hidden.
I climb the stairs and stand where I can see
My child asleep beside her teen magazines,
Her can of Coke, her plate of uncut fruit.
The pomegranate! How did I forget it?

She could have come home and been safe
And ended the story and all
Our heartbroken searching but she reached
Out a hand and plucked a pomegranate.
She put out her hand and pulled down
The French sound for apple and
The noise of stone and the proof
That even in the place of death,
At the heart of legend, in the midst
Of rocks full of unshed tears
Ready to be diamonds by the time
The story was told, a child can be
Hungry. I could warn her. There is still a chance.
The rain is cold. The road is flint-coloured.
The suburb has cars and cable television.
The veiled stars are above ground.
It is another world. But what else
Can a mother give her daughter but such
Beautiful rifts in time?
If I defer the grief I will diminish the gift.
The legend must be hers as well as mine.
She will enter it. As I have.
She will wake up. She will hold
The papery, flushed skin in her hand.
And to her lips. I will say nothing.

At the Glass Factory in Cavan Town

Today it is a swan:
        The guide tells us
these are in demand.
        The glass is made

of red lead and potash
        and the smashed bits
of crystal sinews
        and decanter stoppers

crated over there –
        she points – and shattered
on the stone wheel
        rimmed with emery.

Aromas of stone and
        fire. Deranged singing
from the grindstone.
        And behind that

a mirror – my
        daughters' heads turned
away in it – garnering
        grindstone and fire.

The glass blower goes
        to the furnace.
He takes a pole
        from the earth's

core: the earth's core
       is remembered in
the molten globe at
       the end of it.

He shakes the pole
       carefully to and fro.
He blows once. Twice.
       His cheeks puff and

puff up: he is
       a cherub at the very
edge of a cornice with
       a mouthful of zephyrs –

sweet intrusions into
       leaves and lace hems.
And now he lays
       the rod on its spindle.

It is red. It is
       ruddy and cooler.
It is cool now
       and as clear as

the distances of this
       county with its drumlins,
its herons, its closed-
       in waterways on which

we saw this morning
       as we drove over
here, a mated pair
       of swans. Such

blind grace as they
          floated with told us
they did not know
          that every hour,

every day, and
          not far away from
there, they were
          entering the legend of

themselves. They gave no
          sign of it. But what
caught my eye, my
          attention, was the safety

they assumed as
          they sailed their own
images. Here, now –
          and knowing that

the mirror still holds
          my actual flesh –
I could say to them:
          reflection is the first

myth of loss. But
          they floated away and
away from me as if
          no one would ever blow

false airs on them,
          or try their sinews
in the fire, at
          the core, and they

took no care
        not to splinter, they
showed no fear
        they would end as

this one which is
        uncut yet still might:
a substance of its own
        future form, both

fraction and refraction
        in the deal-wood
crate at the door
        we will leave by.

A Woman Painted on a Leaf

I found it among curios and silver
in the pureness of wintry light.

A woman painted on a leaf.

Fine lines drawn on a veined surface
in a handmade frame.

This is not my face. Neither did I draw it.

A leaf falls in a garden.
The moon cools its aftermath of sap.
The pith of summer dries out in starlight.

A woman is inscribed there.

This is not death. It is the terrible
suspension of life.

I want a poem
I can grow old in. I want a poem I can die in.

I want to take
this dried-out face,
as you take a starling from behind iron,
and return it to its element of air, of ending –

so that autumn
which was once
the hard look of stars,
the frown on a gardener's face,
a gradual bronzing of the distance,

will be,
from now on,
a crisp tinder underfoot. Cheekbones. Eyes. Will be
a mouth crying out. Let me.

Let me die.

Anna Liffey

Life, the story goes,
Was the daughter of Cannan,
And came to the plain of Kildare.
She loved the flatlands and the ditches
And the unreachable horizon.
She asked that it be named for her.
The river took its name from the land.
The land took its name from a woman.

    *

A woman in the doorway of a house.
A river in the city of her birth.

    *

There, in the hills above my house,
The river Liffey rises, is a source.
It rises in rush and ling heather and
Black peat and bracken and strengthens
To claim the city it narrated:
Swans. Steep falls. Small towns.
The smudged air and bridges of Dublin.

    *

Dusk is coming.
Rain is moving east from the hills.
If I could see myself
I would see
A woman in a doorway.
Wearing the colours that go with red hair.
Although my hair is no longer red.

*

I praise
The gifts of the river.
Its shiftless and glittering
Re-telling of a city,
Its clarity as it flows,
In the company of runt flowers and herons,
Around a bend at Islandbridge
And under thirteen bridges to the sea.
Its patience at twilight –
Swans nesting by it,
Neon wincing into it.

*

Maker of
Places, remembrances,
Narrate such fragments for me:

One body. One spirit.
One place. One name.
The city where I was born.
The river that runs through it.
The nation which eludes me.

Fractions of a life
It has taken me a lifetime
To claim.

*

I came here in a cold winter.

I had no children. No country.
I did not know the name for my own life.

My country took hold of me.
My children were born.

I walked out in a summer dusk
To call them in.

One name. Then the other one.
The beautiful vowels sounding out home.

*

Make of a nation what you will
Make of the past
What you can –

There is now
A woman in a doorway.

It has taken me
All my strength to do this.

Becoming a figure in a poem.

Usurping a name and a theme.

*

A river is not a woman.
   Although the names it finds,
      The history it makes
And suffers –
   The Viking blades beside it,
      The muskets of the Redcoats,
         The flames of the Four Courts
Blazing into it –
   Are a sign.
      Anymore than
A woman is a river,
   Although the course it takes,
      Through swans courting and distraught willows,
Its patience
   Which is also its powerlessness,
      From Callary to Islandbridge,
         And from source to mouth,
Is another one.
            And in my late forties
Past believing
      Love will heal
         What language fails to know
And needs to say –
   What the body means –
      I take this sign
And I make this mark:
      A woman in the doorway of her house.
      A river in the city of her birth.
The truth of a suffered life.
      The mouth of it.

   *

The seabirds come in from the coast.
The city wisdom is they bring rain.
I watch them from my doorway.
I see them as arguments of origin –
Leaving a harsh force on the horizon,
Only to find it
Slanting and falling elsewhere.

Which water –
The one they leave or the one they pronounce –
Remembers the other?

I am sure
The body of an ageing woman
Is a memory
And to find a language for it
Is as hard
As weeping and requiring
These birds to cry out as if they could
Recognize their element
Remembered and diminished in
A single tear.

    *

An ageing woman
Finds no shelter in language.
She finds instead
Single words she once loved
Such as 'summer' and 'yellow'
And 'sexual' and 'ready'
Have suddenly become dwellings
For someone else –
Rooms and a roof under which someone else
Is welcome, not her. Tell me,

Anna Liffey,
Spirit of water,
Spirit of place,
How is it on this
Rainy autumn night
As the Irish sea takes
The names you made, the names
You bestowed, and gives you back
Only wordlessness?

     *

Autumn rain is
Scattering and dripping
From carports
And clipped hedges.
The gutters are full.

     *

When I came here
I had neither
Children nor country.
The trees were arms.
The hills were dreams.

I was free
To imagine a spirit
In the blues and greens,
The hills and fogs
Of a small city.

My children were born.
My country took hold of me.
A vision in a brick house.
Is it only love
that makes a place?

I feel it change:
My children are
Growing up, getting older.
My country holds on
To its own pain.

I turn off
The harsh yellow
Porch light and
Stand in the hall.
Where is home now?

Follow the rain
Out to the Dublin hills.
Let it become the river.
Let the spirit of place be
A lost soul again.

    *

In the end
It will not matter
That I was a woman. I am sure of it.
The body is a source. Nothing more.
There is a time for it. There is a certainty
About the way it seeks its own dissolution.
Consider rivers.
They are always en route to
Their own nothingness. From the first moment
They are going home. And so
When language cannot do it for us,
Cannot make us know love will not diminish us,
There are these phrases
Of the ocean
To console us.

Particular and unafraid of their completion.
In the end
Everything that burdened and distinguished me
Will be lost in this:
I was a voice.

Acknowledgements

The poems in this selection are taken from the following books, to whose publishers acknowledgement is made: *Standing Female Nude* (Anvil Press, 1985), *Selling Manhattan* (Anvil Press, 1987), *The Other Country* (Anvil Press, 1990), *Mean Time* (Anvil Press, 1993) and *Selected Poems* (Penguin, 1994) by Carol Ann Duffy; *Close Relatives* (Secker & Warburg, 1981) and *The Handless Maiden* (Jonathan Cape, 1994) by Vicki Feaver; *The War Horse* (Gollancz, 1975), *Night Feed* (Arlen House Press, 1982), *The Journey* (Carcanet Press, 1987), *Outside History* (Carcanet Press, 1990) and *In a Time of Violence* (Carcanet Press, 1994) by Eavan Boland